I Feel Frightened

Written by Brian Moses

Illustrated by Mike Gordon

sundance

Kid-to-Kid Books

Red Set	Green Set	Blue Set	Yellow Set
I Feel Angry	I Feel Bored	I Feel Bullied	Excuse Me!
I Feel Happy	I Feel Jealous	I Feel Frightened	I Don't Care!
I Feel Lonely	I Feel Shy	I Feel Sad	I'll Do It!
It's Not Fair	I Feel Worried	Why Wash?	It Wasn't Me!

All rights reserved.
This edition published
in North America by
Sundance Publishing
P.O. Box 1326
234 Taylor Street
Littleton, MA 01460

First published in 1993 by
Wayland Publishers Limited

Copyright © 1993 Wayland Publishers Limited

ISBN 0-7608-3912-3

Printed in Canada

In the corner today,
we're talking about

feeling frightened.

This way to Kids Corner

3

When I feel frightened, I feel like

quivering jello
on a plate,

a shivering mouse
that's just met a cat,

4

or Little Miss Muffet,
face to face
with a spider.

When I feel frightened,

I put my hands
over my eyes.

I dive under
the covers.

I hide behind
my dad.

7

A lot of things frighten me.
I feel frightened
when I go upstairs alone.

But I tell myself
not to be so silly.
There's nothing there.

Only me!

9

I feel frightened when I think
there are monsters under my bed.

But then I look under the bed,
and there aren't any monsters.

I like to play hide and seek
with my dad.

12

And even though I feel frightened
when Dad makes me jump,
I still want to play it again!

I felt really frightened
on my first day of school.

But I had such a good time
that I didn't want to go home!

The first time I slept at Grandma's house,
I felt frightened.

So Grandma came
and sat on my bed.
She told me stories
until I fell asleep.

My big brother said
that the dentist
was awful.
I felt frightened.

Yikes!

18

But the dentist was nice.
She said I had lovely teeth.

I like to watch scary shows on TV.

Sometimes they frighten me,
but I know they're only make-believe.

When I start to feel frightened,

it helps if I sing
or whistle.

It helps if I tell myself
not to be so silly,

or if I pretend I'm a fearless superhero.

It helps if I talk
to my teddy.

Or if I remind myself
that everyone feels frightened sometimes—
even grown-ups.

My dad hates riding on roller coasters.
He says he feels really frightened.

Mom says she's frightened of flying.
She likes to keep her feet on the ground.

Sometimes when you feel frightened,
you just have to be brave.

What do you do
when you feel frightened?

Write the word *frightened* on a piece of paper. Now list as many words as you can that use only the letters in *frightened*. Stop after two minutes and count how many words you have listed.

How many words can you think of that rhyme with *fright?* List them. Ask a friend to do the same thing. Then compare your word lists.

Find a book that has scary pictures in it. Look at it with a friend. Which picture do you think is the scariest? Which picture does your friend think is the scariest?

List words you might say if something scared you, such as *yikes!*, *yeow!*, or *eek!* Practice saying them the way you would if you really felt scared. Then read the words into a tape recorder. Play the tape and hear yourself sounding scared!

Pretend you are a scary monster. Show a friend how you would walk and what sounds you would make if you were a monster.

my dog

Spat

my house

Other Books to Read

I'm Brave, by Sarah Prince (a Sundance *AlphaKids Guided Reader*, 1999). A girl overcomes her fear of catching the school bus by imagining that she is brave enough to catch fierce creatures. You might also like *Sebastian*, another *AlphaKids Guided Reader* by Sarah Prince. In this book, a shy bird overcomes his fear of school. *12 pages*

Bumps in the Night, by Harry Allard (Bantam, 1979). Scary adventures in a big house are told in a poem. *48 pages*

Franklin in the Dark, by Paulette Bourgeois (Scholastic Books, 1987). Franklin, a turtle afraid of the darkness in his own shell, learns a lesson about fear from his mother. *32 pages*

Little Frog and the Dog, by Martin Waddell (a Sundance *Book Project* book, 1997). Little Frog frightens Auntie Frog, Old Bull Frog, and Sister Frog. Then everyone frightens Little Frog. *16 pages*

A Dark and Stormy Night, by Peter Sloan and Sheryl Sloan (a Sundance *Little Red Reader*, 1996). The animals in a barn have a frightening night when a windy roar sets off a chain of frightened reactions. *8 pages*

Scare and Dare, by Jenny Feely (a Sundance *AlphaKids Guided Reader*, 1999). A boy gets a scary surprise from his older brother, who dares him to go into the scary house at the bottom of the street. *16 pages*

Sheila Rae, the Brave, by Kevin Henkes (Morrow, 1987). When Sheila Rae gets lost on her way home from school, her "scaredy-cat" sister teaches her about bravery. *30 pages*